METAL DRUMMING CONCEPTS

Vital Beats, Exercises, Fills, Tips & Techniques

by Andols Herrick

Cover photo by Mirak Habbiyyieh

ISBN 978-1-4584-0273-8

HAL•LEONARD®
CORPORATION

7777 W. BLUEMOUND RD. P.O. BOX 13819 MILWAUKEE, WI 53213

In Australia Contact:
Hal Leonard Australia Pty. Ltd.
4 Lentara Court
Cheltenham, Victoria, 3192 Australia
Email: ausadmin@halleonard.com.au

Copyright © 2012 by HAL LEONARD CORPORATION
International Copyright Secured   All Rights Reserved

No part of this publication may be reproduced in any form or by any means
without the prior written permission of the Publisher.

Visit Hal Leonard Online at
www.halleonard.com

Acknowledgments

I'd like to thank all of my fans and supporters over the last 12 years for making this effort possible. Thank you to Jeff Schroedl, Debbie Seeger, and everyone from Hal Leonard for the opportunity to make this material available worldwide! Many thanks to Chimaira, for without those years as a band member I would not be so blessed as to have a career as a drummer. Thanks to Chris Spicuzza and Erik Schultek for their major assistance in helping me complete this project. Lastly, thank you to the companies who continue to support my endeavors: Crush, Sabian, Ahead, DB Drum Shoes, Axis, and Evans.

CONTENTS

Thoughts on Practicing

Before we dive into the material, I'd like to take a moment to talk about practicing—more specifically, the difference between *practicing* and *rehearsing*.

What you probably do, more often than not, is rehearse (myself included). Maybe you spend a lot of time playing along with the bands you love, already knowing the drum parts inside and out, just as I did when I was younger. You may have a handful of beats and fills that are your "go-to" material when you are playing for fun. When you are with your band, you are probably drilling your music over and over for an upcoming show or studio session. These are examples of what I consider to be *rehearsing*.

Practicing is a different animal altogether. Say you pick up a drumming magazine, instructional book, or CD, and begin working on a beat that you're unable to play. After an hour of working on it, you're able to play it consistently and accurately. This is *practicing*: you took something you were unable to play, put in the time to work it out, and had developed a new skill.

It's easy to get stuck in a rut with our playing, because what we usually do is rehearse. We don't challenge ourselves with new or more-complicated patterns; rather, we keep using the same old beats and fills, or stay stuck playing at the same speeds. What I hope you'll get out of this book is new inspiration for playing, and that you'll walk away able to play things you were unable to play before.

When you set out to learn a new pattern, begin at a slow tempo. It can seem painfully slow, but whatever speed allows you to play correctly is the right speed. When you are able to play the pattern flawlessly, increase the tempo slightly. Repeat this process until you reach your top speed. This ingrains muscle memory to make performing effortless.

Notation Guide

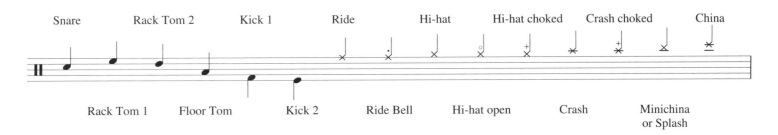

CHAPTER 1:
Double Bass Beat Creativity

As metal drummers, we, of course, do a lot of double bass drumming in the context of our playing. Often, the opportunity presents itself to take a standard double bass beat and spice it up a little bit. What I've done here is written some basic hand patterns with the ride, ride bell, and snare and played them on top of straight double bass. Mixing these patterns into your beats will give your playing a cool groove and break up the monotony.

When you start working on these, get comfortable with the hands before adding the feet. It may take some work to get the coordination down so, as always, start slowly and work your way up in speed. When you get to the accents and ghost notes, really differentiate the loudness of the snare notes. Get a nice big "crack" for the accents. Keep the sticks lower and control the rebound for the quiet ghost notes.

For every pattern, the right hand plays the ride and the left hand plays the snare, except in the half-time snare variation at the end of each page where the right hand will play snare on beat three (instaed of playing ride). Beats two and four become ghost notes and beat three becomes an accented note played by the right hand. (**Note:** The durations of examples on the DVD may differ from the book.)

Patterns (on the DVD)

Pattern #1

Sticking

BUILDING THE BEAT: Step 1

BUILDING THE BEAT: Step 2

BUILDING THE BEAT: Step 3

BUILDING THE BEAT: Step 4

Hands only

Hands and Feet

Half-time Snare

Hands only

R L R R L R L L L R L R R L R L L   R L R R L R L L L R L R R L R L L

Hands and Feet

PUTTING IT ALL TOGETHER

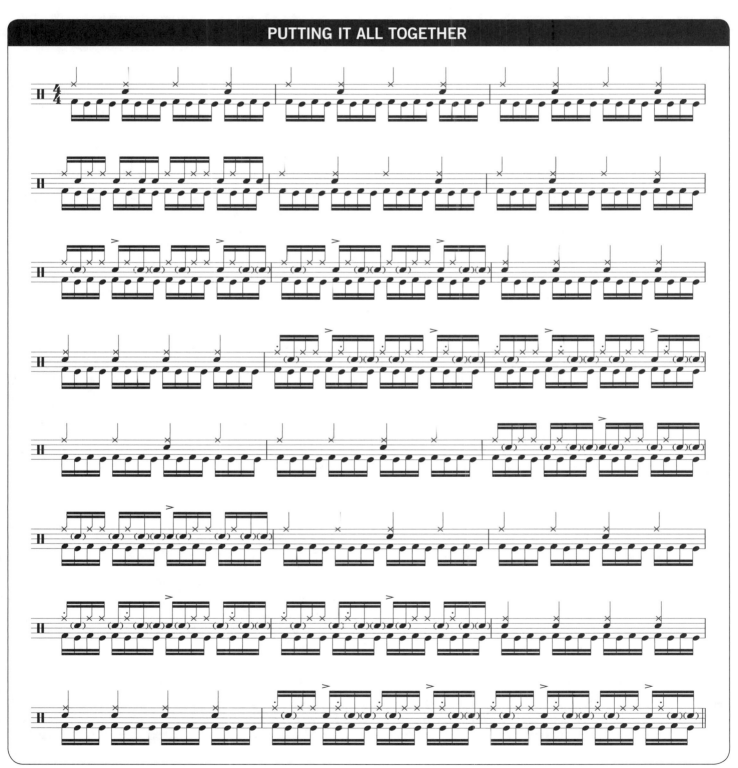

Pattern #2

Sticking

BUILDING THE BEAT: Step 1

BUILDING THE BEAT: Step 2

BUILDING THE BEAT: Step 3

BUILDING THE BEAT: Step 4

Hands only

Hands and Feet

Half-Time Snare

PUTTING IT ALL TOGETHER

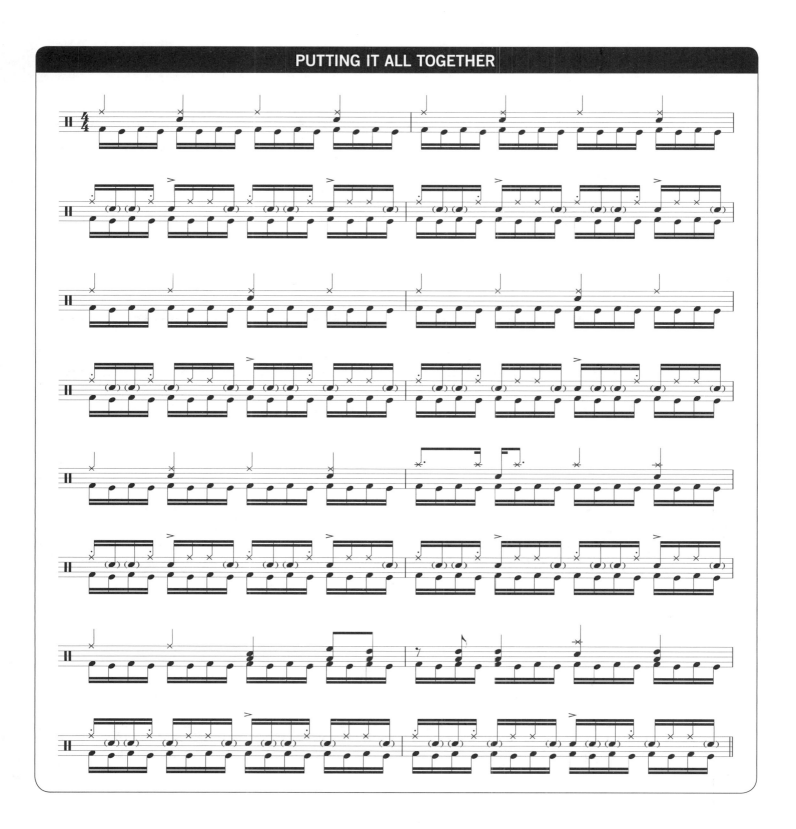

Additional Patterns (not on DVD)

Pattern #3

BUILDING THE BEAT: Step 1

BUILDING THE BEAT: Step 2

BUILDING THE BEAT: Step 3

BUILDING THE BEAT: Step 4

Half-Time Snare

Pattern #4

BUILDING THE BEAT: Step 1

BUILDING THE BEAT: Step 2

BUILDING THE BEAT: Step 3

BUILDING THE BEAT: Step 4

Half-Time Snare

Pattern #5

BUILDING THE BEAT: Step 1

BUILDING THE BEAT: Step 2

BUILDING THE BEAT: Step 3

Half-Time Snare

Pattern #6

BUILDING THE BEAT: Step 1

BUILDING THE BEAT: Step 2

BUILDING THE BEAT: Step 3

BUILDING THE BEAT: Step 4

Half-Time Snare

Pattern #7

BUILDING THE BEAT: Step 1

BUILDING THE BEAT: Step 2

BUILDING THE BEAT: Step 3

BUILDING THE BEAT: Step 4

Half-Time Snare

Pattern #8

BUILDING THE BEAT: Step 1

BUILDING THE BEAT: Step 2

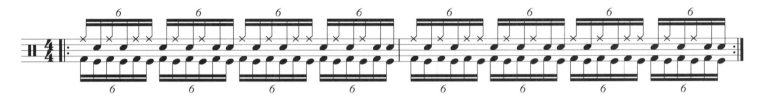

BUILDING THE BEAT: Step 3

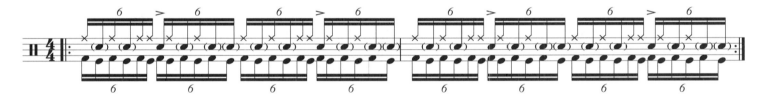

BUILDING THE BEAT: Step 4

Half-Time Snare

CHAPTER 2:
Interval Exercise for Hands

This is a hand exercise inspired by a method in the fitness world called "interval training," which alternates periods of "work" and "rest." For example, a runner will sprint for a short burst, then walk, then sprint again, and so on.

I've applied this idea to drumming by alternating between playing a slow pattern and a fast pattern. If I asked you to play triple strokes or single strokes at your maximum tempo for as long as possible, it wouldn't last particularly long. However, by breaking it up, you can play more at fast tempos and reinforce your ability to play at those speeds.

Something else to think about is *finger control*. While working with students with varying levels of experience, I almost always encounter problems with their hand technique. The faster you play, the more your fingers should take over. If you're holding the stick like you'd grip a dumbbell, your speed will be limited. The following is a three-part explanation of how I demonstrate proper hand technique:

1. The only thing that should be holding the stick is your index finger and thumb. Hold a stick with those two fingers, and no other fingers touching it. Whip the stick down at your practice pad. It should bounce right back up. This is basic physics: equal and opposite reaction. You throw the stick at the pad and the pad throws the stick back up with an equal amount of force. Let the rebound happen. Don't put the brakes on here. Get a feel for the stick moving freely without your other fingers doing anything.

2. Get your other fingers involved in the downward whipping motion. Your middle and ring fingers, while instrumental in the downward motion, should only "be along for the ride" on the rebound. They should touch the stick, but create no resistance. Just let the rebound happen.

3. Once you've mastered the feel of Step 2, you can start to control the rebound. For a clean double stroke, the wrist moves down once, but the fingers pull twice. On the first rebound, your fingers force the stick down a second time, instead of allowing a complete rebound. If you can play a clean double-stroke roll on a dead surface (i.e., a pillow), you've got a firm grasp on what's being described here. The same idea goes for the triple stroke in this exercise. Your wrist should go down once, and your fingers pull three times. The volume of each note should be equal.

It is important to get a good feel for this finger control technique before starting the exercises so you don't ingrain bad habits (i.e., using wrist only) when you're trying to progress.

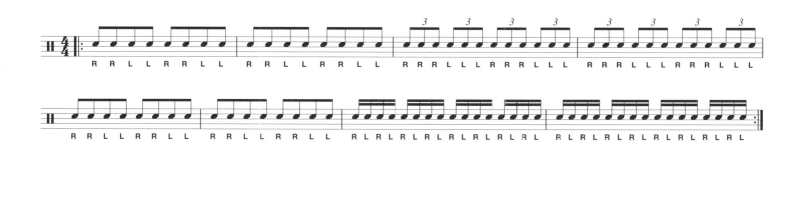

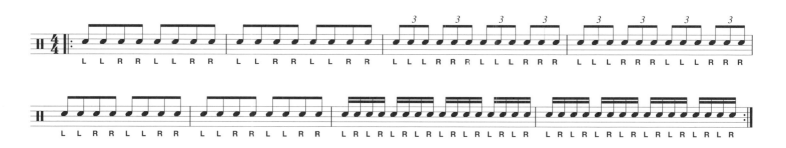

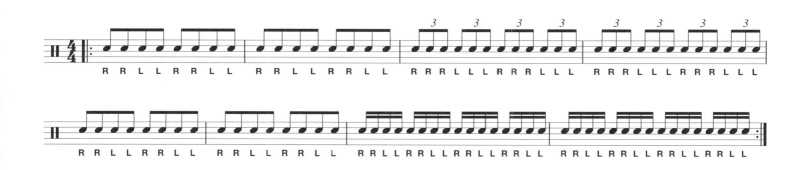

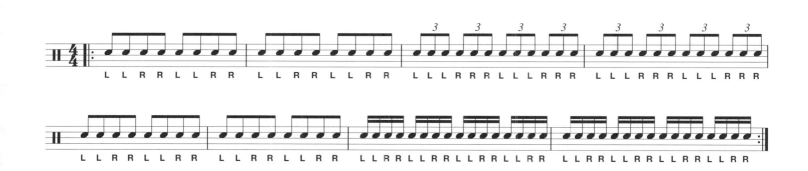

CHAPTER 3:
Time Signature Manipulation

Having a basic understanding of how time signatures work gives you the ability to play around with the feel of a basic 4/4 rhythm. Sometimes odd time signatures seem a bit daunting. Hopefully, we can take the mystique out of them and, in doing so, add some cool ideas for your drum parts.

The first example is a basic 4/4 rock beat. That means the quarter note is the pulse, and there are four quarter notes in a measure. Four quarter notes take up the same amount of time as eight eighth notes.

Counting Example #1

COUNTING A MEASURE: Step 1 (4/4)

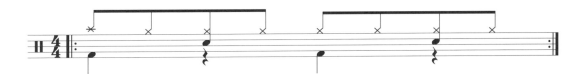

If we chop off that last eighth note, our pattern would be in 7/8. That means the eighth note is the pulse, and there are seven eighth notes per measure. When counting in seven, say "sev" instead of "seven." This makes counting easier. It also avoids the potential error of playing an extra beat with the extra syllable.

COUNTING A MEASURE: Step 2 (7/8)

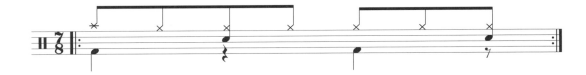

Let's look at another example, this time with toms and double bass. **Note:** In preparation for the conversion to 7/8, you may try counting in eight.

Counting Example #2

COUNTING A MEASURE: Step 1 (4/4)

Here's the same pattern cut to 7/8. To make it fit we cut the equivalent of one eighth note (two sixteenth notes take up the same space as one eight note).

COUNTING A MEASURE: Step 2 (7/8)

"Pictures in the Gold Room"

Now that we've practiced some odd-time patterns, we can move to the example from the Chimaira song "Pictures in the Gold Room." What I've done here is take 32 beats total, but instead of playing a straight 4/4 groove throughout, I decided to take some liberties with the bar line. There are five different patterns here: four patterns are in 7 (making 28 beats), and one pattern is in 4 (for a total of 32 beats). Everything is broken down section by section.

Pattern #1

Pattern #2

With cymbals

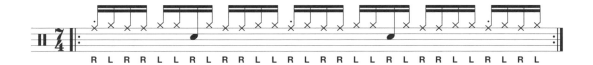

R L R R L L R L R R L L R L R R L L R L R R L L R L R L

With kick matching ride bell

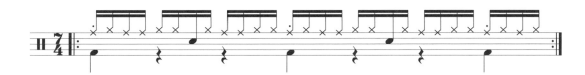

Patterns #1 and #2

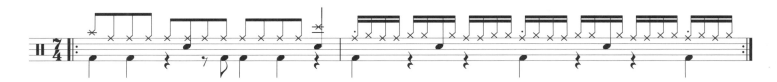

Pattern #3

Patterns 1–3

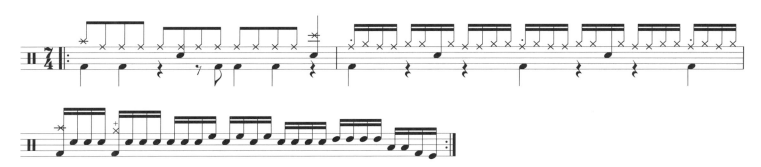

Pattern #4

Patterns 1–4

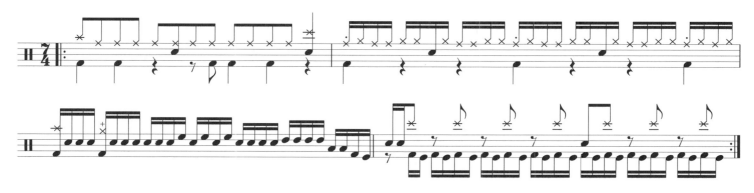

Pattern #5

Patterns 1–5

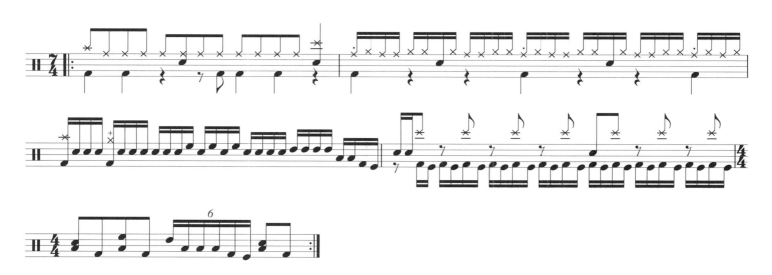

I created an alternate drumset part, just to give you an idea of a different way to break it down. Any grouping will work if the total number of beats equals 32 for this particular example. This one consists of the time signatures 5/4, 7/4, 4/4. Give it a shot!

Alternate Pattern (not on DVD)

CHAPTER 4:
Developing the Blast Beat

I n the grand scheme of my drumming life, I'm relatively new to the blast beat, so I can relate to those of you who struggle with it. I had issues with the coordination between hands and feet, and more specifically not having them start to flam together. Getting the snare to play exactly between the kicks can be tricky at first. The snare is so syncopated you can lose the beat.

Here are some exercises I practiced when first learning to blast. I am by no means a blast beat master, but I can offer some help as someone who struggled with them like you may be doing right now. We'll begin by alternating between a two-bar double-bass beat and a two-bar blast. After you get comfortable and solid with that, we'll double the length of each. Finally, we'll get more advanced by adding ride bell and china.

Basic Blast Beat

1. Two-bar blast

2. Four-bar blast

Cymbal Variations

The variations can also be practiced as four-bar blasts.

1. Ride bell

2. China

3. China and ride bell

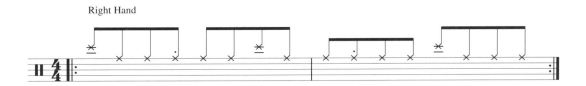

4. Four-bar blast

5. Blast option

Triplet Blast Beats

Now let's try some examples with a triplet feel. These can be even trickier if you're like me and play a double-kick blast as opposed to a single-foot blast. The right and left feet alternate landing on the beat, which can cause problems with the feel. We'll start with the same idea as the sixteenth note blasts by alternating between a backbeat and a blast. Then we'll add the ride bell.

1. Triplet blast

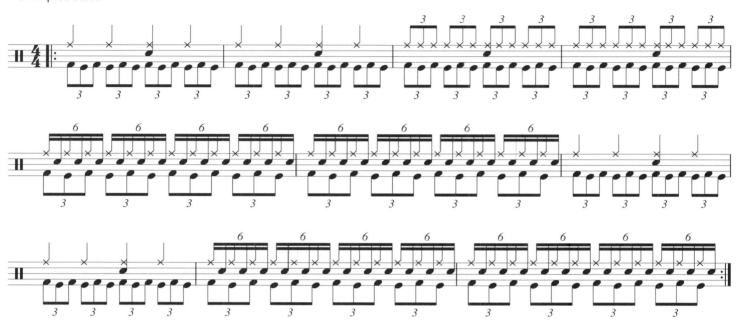

2. Ride bell

CHAPTER 5:
Fills with Cymbal Clenches

In the next two chapters, we're going to work on ideas to give your drum fills new life. Throwing in some cymbal clenches (also known as chokes) in your fills can add some variety. You can accent spots that really make the fill stand out.

When you get comfortable with the fills, use them with some double bass beats. For example, play three bars of a double bass beat and then play a fill, and repeat. Focus on a smooth transition from the beat into the fill, and the fill back into the beat. Once you get solid with these examples, you can start applying them to your own playing. Think about spots where the fills can match what the guitar is playing when you're working on parts for your own music.

For the clenches themselves, don't choke the cymbal too early or too late. It should have a quick, sharp attack and then be choked firmly.

Fills with Clenches (on the DVD)

1. Clench on Beat 1

2. Clench on Beat 2

3. Clench on Beat 3

4. Advanced Two-Bar Fill

Additional Fills (not on DVD)

1.

2.

3.

4.

5.

6.

7.

8.

9.

10.

CHAPTER 6:
Fills with Hi-hat Chokes

H i-hat chokes are another way to give your fills a new sound. Hi-hat chokes are played by striking the open hi-hat, and then quickly closing the hi-hat with the foot. For the fills in this chapter, close the hi-hat at the same time you play the next sixteenth note.

I really like fills with hi-hat chokes on "e" and "a." It creates a cool syncopated feel. The left hand can play the hi-hat on "e" and "a", so the right-hand crossover is not required. When your right hand has to cross over to the hi-hat, it limits you options. If you're lucky enough to have a remote hi-hat (which I unfortunately do not), you have more possibilities when adding hi-hat chokes.

Presented here are eight fills, each with five variations. Get comfortable with these fills and explore other possibilities on your own.

Sticking Guide

C	=	Crash and Kick Drum
L	=	Left Hand
R	=	Right Hand
H	=	Hi-hat and Kick Drum
r	=	Ride and Kick Drum
M	=	Minichina/Splash and Kick Drum

Example 1

C L R L R L R L H L R L R L R L C

A.

B.

C.

D.

Example 2

C L R L R L R L R H R L R L R L C

A.

B.

C.

D.

Example 3

C   L   R   L   R   L   H   L   H   L   R   L   R   L   R   L   C

A.

B.

C.

D.

Example 4

C L R L R L R H R H R L R L R L C

A.

B.

C.

D.

Example 5

C L R L R L H L H L R L H L R L C

A.

B.

C.

D.

Example 6

C L R L R L R H R H R L R H R L C

A.

B.

C.

D.

Example 7

C   L   R   L   R   L   H   L   L   H   L   L   H   L   R   L   C

A.

B.

C.

D.

Example 8

C L R L R L H L L H L L H L R L C   C

A.

B.

C.

D.

CHAPTER 7

Applied Drum Fills

In this chapter, I'll show you how I utilized the ideas from Chapters 5 and 6 in some of my own work. I think it's important to learn how these ideas may be applied, rather than just seeing them as exercises. Hopefully, this will help you incorporate them into your own playing situations.

The first example comes from the song "Six." It incorporates the hi-hat chokes from Chapter 6.

Example 1: "Six" (3:04 into song)

The second example incorporates the hi-hat choke in a slightly different context. Since I am left-handed, I tend to lead with my left hand and left foot when playing quads. In Example 2, I play the first rack (left hand) followed by the floor tom (right hand), and then the second rack followed by the floor tom. Since most of you are right-handed, this can be tricky. An alternative is to play two notes on each rack tom so the right hand can lead. The hi-hat closes on the downbeat with the bass drum and crash.

Example 2: "Six" (3:21 into song)

The third example demonstrates the use of a cymbal clench on the "and" of beat 3. I am a fan of accenting the off-beat.

Fill Example 3: "Six" (3:40 into song)

The last example comes from the tune "Implements of Destruction." This fill is one of my personal favorites. I've broken this down into steps. First, practice the hand pattern, and then add the kick drum. After that, work on the right hand moving between the crash, hi-hat, and ride bell.

Example 4: "Implements of Destruction" (7:49 into song)

STEP 1: Sticking Pattern

STEP 2: Add kick drum

STEP 3: Floating right hand

STEP 4: Hi-hat choke

PUTTING IT ALL TOGETHER

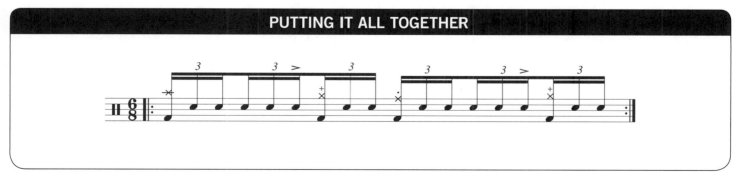

CHAPTER 8:
Paradiddle-diddle Exercise

This hand technique exercise will get you comfortable with the paradiddle-diddle rudiment and help develop speed. Like the interval exercise in Chapter 2, it alternates between a slow pattern and a fast pattern. This exercise uses accents and the paradiddle-diddle to further develop finger control.

The goal is to differentiate between the accented and non-accented notes. You will need to have developed the ability to control the rebound as discussed in Chapter 2. The double strokes need to be played evenly and quieter than the accented notes.

The sixteenth-notes are all paradiddle-diddles except the last two which fill out the measure.